AF762408

Another Anthem of Fabulous Survival

POETIC JUSTICE INSTITUTE

Elisabeth Frost, *series editor*

Another Anthem of Fabulous Survival

T.S. Leonard

foreword by Meg Day

Fordham University Press   New York   2026

Fordham University Press also publishes its books in a variety of electronic formats. Some content that appears in print may not be available in electronic books.

Visit us online at www.fordhampress.com.

For EU safety / GPSR concerns: Mare Nostrum Group B.V., Doelen 72, 4831 GR Breda, The Netherlands, gpsr@mare-nostrum.co.uk

Library of Congress Cataloging-in-Publication Data available online at https://catalog.loc.gov.

Printed in the United States of America

28 27 26 5 4 3 2 1

First edition

for my father,
who taught me how to sing

Contents

Foreword

I've been wishing for a book like this. In this kairotic moment, I'm looking for poetry that does something, that verbs: it startles or archives, turns my head or challenges my poetics. The poems in *Another Anthem of Fabulous Survival* do much more than this, and they do it with deadpan humor and dramatic irony, brazen insistence and a keen eye on the sociocultural ignorance erasure ensures. What's more, these poems—like so many generations of queer folks—are formally inventive and deeply, seriously playful without ever losing sight of the stakes.

Another Anthem of Fabulous Survival manages to not only address inequity, compelling action and reflection on behalf of marginalized experiences, but to perform the most dangerous thing of all: sustaining joy in the midst of crisis, absolute life in the face of death. We need this book, especially in this sociocultural and political moment, because it is edifying, yes—but also because it insists on a future still ambivalent about being born.

Meg Day, Poetic Justice Institute Prize Judge, 2024–2025

pleasure in hard times gives us relief
until we all belong to the song

—CAConrad

Another Anthem of Fabulous Survival

Search Engine

When it starts up, the end hissesss . . .
a wheel of sparks and seconds peeling
back, revealing minutes. Then the entire bar
starts to rattle, sings along. Every line snags;

it sounds like Saturday, the century opening
a hole through the roof. Stars spill in, now
everybody's moving, unaware the present
already is ending. This is why we dance:

keeping time, back & forth. The floor cracks
down its middle, all our pasts pool below;
some folks dive in. Or grab on, the chrome
ark exploding now skyward, its mirror ball tail

an arc of repeated light. It all starts to blur:
what once was community has become a server;
lopsided daisies cover ruins, circuitry. Blasting past
disco, diseases, salt, dynasties: all tracks on a busted

jukebox. Past new wave dancers now overgrown
by flowering thyme, or a pastel rubble. Everybody
goes, and comes. The place collapses. It skips,
the record tries to keep up. That's the joke:

the bartender says, I'm sorry,
we don't serve time travelers here.
A time traveler crashes into a gay bar.

[/]

Sidekicks Saloon

It's not just a gay bar, it's a country
western gay bar in Kansas City,

Missouri—see the busted neon boot
open sign and barn red barstools; long

since before straight couples said *partner*,
Sidekicks has been home to hustlers and

queens, hogging up all the pretty fellas
playing pretend billiards; sass a lonesome

cowpoke, charm the traveling oil baron,
learn to two-step from two women

both called Linda: *honey, let me tell ya,*
we have to be twice as quick as the men.

I wreck the dancefloor sawdust,
watching myself and the dirty mirror

makes everything two times bigger;
and I reckon I do look lonely tonight.

Outside, there's a storm kicking up
and gusts rattle the saloon doors,

but I like how the two swing, split
down the middle: half-shut, half-open.

The Time Traveler Hears Music for the First Time

Reader, it sounds like sex with the angels. Open
our entire mouths, animal tongues bouncing—
the cave quivers, reliving each echo of our low
howl; I am hooked. My abdomen a golden harp,
my appetite plucked. Gods get thanked. Wars
pause. Lovers make peace with their ends. Next,
we start to dance: our hips the lyrics, translating
sound to circles. Doing the twist. Imitating thunder,
we thump a tempo on our knees. We craft a flute
from salvaged bones. Use rubble for drums. Make
grief into a fiddle, and strum. Entire symphonies
rise from ash, loss. Reader, my whole ass is shaking;
my head-holes feel finally full. Cue the horns! More
ancient than memory, this rhythm is all we have
ever known: it pleases the muses, and our cave
fills with pulsing bass. Walls shake. It's a disco,
a dance floor mixing gods and men, music is—
an eternity. Reader, does any song have to
end? And if I can use my throat for singing,
isn't every breath, then, a possible infinity?

Autobiography in the Tracklist of Blue

1. I am born blue and wanted, with an uncomplicated and all-consuming desire: to devour everything; to change.
2. My old man loved Joni Mitchell, and thank god, I got my soft heart from him.
3. When I was a little boy, I said green was my favorite color. I said Spring was my favorite season. I said future was my favorite tense. When you are young, finality comes easy. A choice is just a choice, then, not a constellation of possible losses.
4. I didn't go to Morocco when I had the chance. I missed my flight to Madrid. I slept through Spring semester and smoked a thousand cigarettes each night. My boyhood bloomed wrong and rowdy, so I taught myself how to dance.
5. My old man's soft heart stopped beating when I was a freshman. I learned how to be lonely.
6. I drove to California on the last of my dad's life insurance. My last May in Missouri it was raining every day, so I dreamed up Los Angeles. I didn't realize what I was looking for was already gone. To want anything is a desire to be changed.
7. If I weren't so afraid of flying, I would be a bluebird. I, too, sing when I get scared. I would glide over the floodplains of my boyhood and survey what's been lost.

8. The LA River is drying up, its concrete vein now a fossil of its former self. A memory of a revision of what used to be a free-flowing stream. The Missouri River is called Big Muddy; it erodes its own banks and carries the silt along with it where it runs.

9. Me, I leave too easily and love too hard. I meet a man who's perfect for me, and the next day I have already grown away. But if I had to choose one album to bring to a desert island, I'm sure it would be this one.

10. I don't remember the last time I saw my old man because I didn't know it would be the last time. I had just told him I liked other boys, and he said that he was worried, the world is hard enough as it is. If I could reach him now, I would tell him that it's been okay. I would tell him how I have known love. I would tell him about California, and how Joni was right about the river. I would tell him that my favorite color now is blue, and I think I would want nothing more.

Cyclone Scene Haibun

She runs quickly from the fortune teller. Green sky quiet as a priest. A good listener. No concern kicking up dust in her beat-up, prairie plain shoes. Flopping pigtails. One-eyed storm looms high up over tallgrass. Cocks and hens coax gusts along with them into the coop. They squawk, and the sky answers. It's that time of the year when she cracks up. Whirls. Whips wind and tears apart the sepia landscape. Secretly, she is thrilled—what will come after this all gets torn away? First, a door rips open. Next, a beam. Her bedroom window comes flying; after it, the screen. Auntie screams. Outside, everything she knows passes by: her uncle and his impish grin, the chickens and their chicken pen, her nemesis. This longing for an obscene change. Like a movie, she watches that old life twist away. Vanish. And the busted house lands with a thud. A door creaks open, cautious, onto a painted valley. Who can she be here? She steps through it. She gets a fresh new pair of kicks. She decides to stay.

blue sky on gold brick
spring in emerald city lush
now she dreams of storms

the time traveler's blues [i n t e r l u d e]

in my line I fall in love & lose someone every time I clock in
chasing that tornado 'til it twirls inside out—an hourglass
the thing about leaving is leaving everyone behind
I click my heels & scream *home* 'til I'm hoarse
& still it won't bring back the early dead
I carry all my chickenhearted friends
into all my imperfect future pasts
I click my heels & scream *home*
whirling 'til my ankles bleed
I try to dance you back
they ruby & go on &
still you're gone
& still you're
gone &
still

All These Years of Loss Have Learned Me

Run at life like a hungry animal. When you reach water,
watch its body divide. Make yourself large and loud—
scream, if necessary. Even in blizzards, tears won't freeze;
hold on to small things. If you don't believe in ghosts or
angels, you put faith, instead, in memories. Pay close
care to laughter. There comes a clear winter morning
when you wake up and you don't think of him at all—
this will be the worst part of grief: the loss of loss.
Everything is a process. It takes about ninety minutes
to cremate a human body. What happens to molecules
upon cremation is what happens to molecules every day:
we change, drift away, rejoin the atmosphere. Wear purple
if it helps you remember. Or denim. You will become many
unrecognizable versions of yourself. You have to believe
he would have loved them all. He will morph, too,
become reef beacon; become first snow. The same few
stories—all you have—can be turned over and over
and, like tumbled jasper, will uncover soft new edges.
There will be a clear winter morning when you wake,
crying, because you thought you could hear him sing.
This will be the best part of grief: how it refuses to forget
you, even after all this time. Tracks buried from the drift.

Love Song

The man I love will be a mother
fucking monster, a milky sea with a heart
the size of a whale. A whole season of a person;
he'll change. He will be my sister

in the sense that our love makes him
cry easily. Like us across the Badlands watching
clouds break, the man I love will be a storm:
he'll form, he'll fury, and I will remain

a prairie.

[///]

Instructions for Building Your First Time Machine

Don't. The past is overcrowded with the future
closer than you think. You blink, that's one
eon; a yawn, two. Take a few photographs—
one of your mother, some of your childhood,
one of the most embarrassing fashion mistakes
you made in your twenties—stack them up,
shuffle, deal. Fixate on some thoughtless crack
you made at that party, years ago. You will live
to make another. You will live again. Try reflecting
a mirror to another mirror—watch yourself
replicate endlessly. Try breaking. Paste those
shards onto a globe; now you've made a disco
ball—change! Step one: forget everything;
step two: forget step one. Step one-two-three:
if you're just dancing here that's good enough;
when the music stops, stay where you are—
you're older now than you ever imagined;
you remember wanting to forget. You didn't.
Keep walking away from the wreckage.

Hooray For You

The world works—and doesn't—in mysterious ways.

//

When I was young, all I wanted was to be a big star.
Now, all I want is to go to bed. I came out, like a sucker,

to California, to write for the movies; I got a job writing
slam reviews of diet supplements for a Russian troll farm
right under the *D* in the Hollywood sign.

\\

Nothing we do is ever enough—thank god,
can you imagine how boring that would be?

//

There are seasons in Los Angeles, and loneliness, too.
That June Gloom, I was sneaking into the Hollywood Roosevelt
pool, reading Joan Didion, pretending to be someone.

I was working for a defense attorney in Beverly Hills,
ordering salads and reviewing cases of gruesome sexual assault.
Driving home, I would sing to the radio at the top of my lungs.

\\

You can't go back,
   you can only go farther.

//

   That June, after a man killed 49 people at a gay club
called Pulse, I didn't want to be alone. I went down
to City Hall for a vigil, thousands of little candles,

and afterward marched over to a gay club called Precinct
with dozens of other strangers. They were playing
Paris Is Burning on the big screen. We quoted along:

\\

CLOSE UP Dorian Corey is applying her face,
eyes on herself in the mirror, reflecting on her
life in the ballroom. *I always had hopes of being*
a big star . . . , she says, *and as you get older you*
aim a little lower. She raises a pencil to her right
eyebrow. *Then you think you left a mark on the*
world if you just get through it . . . and a few people
remember your name. She pats her cheeks carefully.
Pay your dues and enjoy it. She does not look at the

camera, she doesn't have to. *If you shoot an arrow*
and it goes real high, hooray for you.

//

I left Los Angeles at the end of July, tail between
my legs, everything I owned in my trunk. Once I reached
Oregon, a stranger said she could get me a job:

Pretty much I teach kids about art, she explained,
then go home and smoke weed in my bathtub.
So I stayed.

\\

Time, the arrow, like success, or fame:
we only see its course in reverse,
and chase its arc, its arc—
a history of rainbows.

Dancing Queen

funny, not ha-ha, but when Dad died we watched
Mamma Mia! in the living room and cracked up
for the first time in a week. Thanks, Meryl Streep.
It was sudden. Mom's friend brought us the DVD;
sister sang along. And I had heard the line wrong,
thought: *You can dance, you can die.* I was young,
not sweet, barely eighteen. Too cool for ABBA.
My idea of fun, then, was finding strange men
old enough to be my father who I could pick up;
suck their limp pricks in the park. Go home high,
find Dad awake: ice cream scoop, a book, his trust
I would make good decisions. Small things you miss.
See that boy turn bastard. Watch that father reverse
dance away. Hold him, if you get the chance. Release.

the time traveler's finale [s k i t]

The Summer I Was Kurt von Trapp

I was twelve going on thirteen. The fireflies
were brighter than the streetlamps. All my friends
were in the chorus, playing Nazis and nuns. The war
on terror had just begun. The actor playing the
Captain was seventeen going on eighteen—

he left rehearsals in his Jetta, the Mother Superior
riding shotgun. Cackling into the dark. We ran through
"Do-Re-Mi" over and over, bobbing up and down. We
saw on the news IEDs bloom in night-vision green.
I went to Boy Scout camp and wanted to die.

I went to rehearsal every night in July;
the Captain barking at us, again and again.
We had to get it right. His voice in my ear,
I masturbated for the first time, writhing
on the cold bathroom floor. On the news

we saw priests sinning, getting caught. I was sweating
through my gray sailor suit. We went out for slushies after
tech. Empty Sonic. I watched the Captain lick his blue lips.
I wanted him to watch me, and I knew that it was wrong.
Closing night, we made a circle: the Captain's shoulder

touching mine. He sang about a clean, bright flower.
We pretended to escape. Hiding in the wings,
it came over me: an understanding. Easy.
I knew, now, what I wasn't—
I knew who I was supposed to be.

The Time Traveler Tries Drag

It's almost time to go on, and thank god—
she craves the almost. If she could replicate

that edge—those edges—between becoming
winged, or wigged, she would sing. Her lips go

last, a violent red. A just-right lash. She adjusts
her tuck, fixes her hips. Soaks up all this flux

and listens—she is next. *For the first time,*
please give it up for Miss Milly Second!

[/ It's 1893 and she could get arrested for this.

/ It's 1963 and she could get arrested for this.

/ It's 2026 and she could get arrested for this.]

It's half-past eleven and the whole place erupts,
vibrating with delicious want. They, too, crave

her almost, her power: to be so brave to dance
along the ridges of a visible shift. They cheer

as she reveals a nude illusion. She catches [herself
as a young man, vanishing into the crowd—

inside of him, like everyone, is a raging want
to survive] all the ones, her roses; she changes

offstage [listening for sirens]. The future almost here.

A National Anthem

The last time some man called me a faggot, mountains sang:
a bird called America blushed, devoured roses. The thorns
stuck in her teeth, like tough bits of meat. He got in my face.
I did not blink. I sang back to my country, a quilt of torn flags;
his hiss hung around my lips. His breath stank. Dogwoods
bloomed pink above us. My father's father's mother plucked
a folk ballad on catfish bones. The Ozarks wept and bled mud
waterfalls, wagons broke. He said, know what that makes you?
Goddamn unamerican. His snout nearly brushing mine. Dirt
behind his eyes. My country, whose violences I cannot shake—
whose purple pumps through my veins— whose song sticks
in my lungs— whose nasty history of who owns whom is no more
his than mine— then this country, too, is a faggot. He should be
so lucky as to have a name. To have a changing flag and a history
of plague and dancing. A whole prairie shivered. He stood still.
The last time some man called me a faggot, I became a nation.

a national anthem (7”) [o u t r o]

a bird called America

her teeth, tough bits of meat

quilt of torn flags;

hung around my lips

pink above us plucked

wept and bled

waterfalls

nearly brushing

his eyes violences I cannot shake—

changing flag a history

a faggot a nation.

Over the Rainbow

Left the house today only to find everything
outside was exactly the same. It's beautiful,
but sometimes I do miss the sepia.

When I was a boy I wanted nothing
more than to slam my body into Kansas
and come out dancing on the other side.

Every time it rains, I cry. I try to
cover myself in bluebird feathers and flap
both my arms, failing once again to fly.

A beloved diva, having risen from the provinces to
the grand stage of La Scala, tells me: most if not all of
life is waiting in the wings.

She pouts her lips and chides, *you came all this way*
just to keep having the same dream? She's got a point.
Lately, when it pours, I pray for patience. Waiting

for rainbows, I try to count the colors as they pass:
strawberry fingers, traffic cone, pissing in the trough;
palm limbs, powder blue dawn, you in vintage denim;

and tomorrow, drooping like wisteria. I could stand
to learn a thing or two from my gone wishes.
I do my best now to bend.

[////]

and coming upon the cave, I can hear hymn / after hymn of disco scripture / echo off the dark / open mouth: *I will survive*; / *I feel love—* / I do not feel / alone; behind me, / my ghosts my guides; / I coax a chorus of gone tenors / to begin; I sing into the cave // because gardenias are far too brief / because figs, too, fall and rot / because we do not know the end / of every dark edge / because some queens even get buried with their wigs / we sing, too, to remember / the words // I write to last. // and the dark ages must come / just before renaissance / and nobody knows the end / of any song until it's gone / as it began: in silence. / I am before / the dark beginning, ghosts behind me / ghosts to come / and maybe this is not absence, it is merely one moment until
another song begins . . . // [. . .] ///

"Halo"

The first time we visit a bathhouse together
in the second decade of our long & changing
friendship, I pass you pressed against a wall
getting head from a bald man. We exchange
a glance that is also a history. You can't come.
We laugh about it. Later, the world ends
& we get buzzcuts. We get high, hold hands
all through the finale. You know what makes me
break into tears, you, the one who made me.
I watch you shit on FaceTime, I see you change
in real time, I know you're tired but Girl!!!
you can't leave, I don't know who I'd be
without you. The world ends, again,
& we go out dancing. You in your pink box
braids, the best of us twisted up on the floor
of the empire, you in your gold
afro looking like a saint
candle, flickering to the beat,
the way I see you in my memory
when I need to feel free, I leave
voice memos on my best friend's phone
like bitch, you're so famous,
keep on surviving—

& the next time you forget the words,
won't you call my name?
& if the world is really ending now
isn't friendship also
a prayer?

the time traveler's lament [i n t e r l u d e]

what do you call nostalgia for a past nostalgia? A song that samples a song that samples a song about a one-night stand. What do you call nostalgia for a time that hasn't yet passed? Hope? Someday this will all be a memory, and the queens in small town Kansas will need to know how we dressed. How we kissed. How we fought. How we fight. How we remember.

In These Uncertain Times

our friends move to the country and the country is called the past

we watch patiently for deer and beg for their forgiveness

I can't sleep unless I'm supposed to be at work

I do and do not dream of labor

we forget how to talk about the weather

someone is falling in love for the first time

someone is learning how to grieve

borders blur in the pouring rain

we make feasts from food stamps and candles out of straws

I grow nostalgic for a different emergency

it's not the heat that'll get you, or the humidity, it's something we have not yet felt

we are barreling headlong into our bygones

survival is a starved animal

survival is an ugly, gorgeous thing

the orcas are organizing against the rich

a sense of belonging opens like a fist

a symphony of seventeen-year cicadas scores pride

again everyone wants to sound like disco

our friends help their friends pay the rent

our friends help their friends move

cow burps are another leading cause

there is no outrunning change

there is no cover at the tea dance

we confuse the thunderclaps for a throbbing bass

we try to seize both the fruit and the weed

I'm already homesick for the holocene

the only light is the glow of the screen

I can't sleep until I have seen everything

we take a walk in another wildfire

epochs dissolve like salt

we watch the crisis unfold in real time

the word livestream does not mean river

I catch death tolls in my teeth like a bear

someone is learning how to fish

someone is learning how to do the butterfly

everything morphs each time you push the pool away

each time a heart beats it is remembering how

I scrub my palms raw and sing happy birthday to no one

our friends help their friends pay for surgery

survival is a seven-minute dance song

in the blur we forget how to remember

we watch our friends exchange vows in another country

we are all of us in boxes

we watch ourselves make a face

we fuck like animals over text

the white-crowned sparrows start to sing louder

a record year for rainfall causes flooding, and a superbloom

I clog the drain with rose petals and rosemary trying to relax

the bullfrog's croak is getting shorter in the heat

a burning library is not a metaphor

we make a plan for what we could grab

mostly, we look back on what was gentle

everyone has their own strange dreams

we have thanksgiving over facetime

we make fish for new year's eve

I make a list of what I hope to change

the sirens start to sound like music

operating manual for the time traveler [s k i t]

OPERATING MANUAL FOR THE TIME TRAVELER
U.S. DEPT. OF TRANSPORTATION
[REDACTED]

When the switchover occurs [redacted]
by an angle [redacted]
between the two
trajectories. This is [redacted]
not performed [redacted] the
switchover has occurred [redacted]
continue to be computed [redacted]
shortly after touchdown [redacted]
the landing shock will not disrupt [redacted]
attitude [redacted] nor will the [redacted] change [redacted]
(by settling or
shifting) [redacted] the attitude is stored. [redacted]

Earth, Wind, and Mostly Fire

On a rare warm day in San Francisco, I met a philosopher
(I know, *I know*) writing a book about the classical elements

—earth, air, water, fire—which she said needed revision.
I don't know if there's a new one, or a dropped one, like Destiny's

Child, or if one (maybe fire?) gets brought to the front, like Diana
Ross to the Supremes. Or for that matter, Beyoncé. I can't say

if I even grasp carbon emissions. All I know is that she has
 a point: shit's changing. We're gonna need a bigger

 definition: a planet is a girl group. Earth is not a star.

And yes, things are heating up. [Insert forest here] is on fire.

"Everything's on fire" is now a common greeting.

Beyoncé on the radio sings "I'm lookin' for a new foundation,"
 seconds after announcing she's just quit her job.

The song of the summer is the sound of collective resignation
 to our new hot doom. A shake-up in the lineup looms.

The problem with apocalyptic thinking is how it prizes endings.
Darling, I hate to break it to you, but life will go on—

perhaps unrecognizably—and maybe that's scarier than all of this
smoke. Change is hot. I mean hard. Like mud, or wind,

or maybe we'll be dazzled by the talents of a new element,
another anthem of fabulous survival. We will learn
all the words, trying our best to sing along.

Fairyland

an old friend is a bullet
train straight to your past
spread out on a woven rainbow

throw in the dirt we found
a half-sun spot in between
the mirror lake and Fairyland

if they could see us now
they being us but back then
all our old parts on shuffle

OJ and champagne Oakland
Wednesday midday all hazy
32 and 35 and 33 we sang

Mary J. Blige and we survived
Florida Georgia Kansas our bodies
playlists perfectly sequenced and shared

messy goat cheese and bullshit
since the whole-ass last pandemic
we have moved we keep moving

back from the sun a bit we laugh
who we were before we met
who we were on the internet

who is going to remember all of this
walking back to the car we are belting
"Real Love" when a stranger joins in

a notes app joke a triptych photo
strip a wig reveal and we search on
next track next era next shape another one

Every Friend a Lightbulb

after Felix González-Torres's "Untitled (America #1)" (1992)

Coiled pile, cord bunched on the floor,
light bulbs heaped into a nest, and the rest,   fifteen more,
        climbing a long string toward the ceiling,
        each light reaching—feeling—up and
away from its mess, but still tethered,
even floating, back to the ground
        and its brothers, by the same thread.
        Each light, eventually, blinks out.
Now I stand before the sculpture and picture
how it must feel to lose fifteen friends:
        Michael and the way he says, *oh my god;*
Max and with him the secrets to the world's best khoresht;
Chip's inimitable voices and Kathleen's sass
and Mollie when they get excited;
Thea in her studio; Damani in his Beyoncé wig;
Rory when she clicks her tongue, or organizes marches;
            Hunter, how we read, even how we fight;
            Nurse Minh in his nurse drag;
                Savannah in their Easter best,
                    Brian's singing;
                        Nora's plans;
                            Peter;
                        Paige;
                            ;

Love Will Tear Us Apart (12")

a long life is a myth
you used to joke
invented by the insurance
industry to sell more
life: you were the funny one
and I was proud just to be
an audience, your friend.
We grew up in the same
forgotten place in the plains,
and I was your mother
and I was your son
and you were my country
back when we had none.
Toward the end, we blew up
a hundred pink balloons
just to watch our breath
fill their round bodies,
stringing streamers
all over the living
room where you lived
up to your self-given title
of midnight movie idol
posing for my camera:
I took a hundred pictures
and in none of them are you
standing still

would you remember now
the night we tried to break
into the art museum
because you had to piss,
you insisted, on the Martyrdom
of Saint Sebastian but would settle
for a cute guard on night shift;
he wasn't amused by this
but you got away with it
like you did everything
by having the most
piercing grin
this side of the state
line and we were lying
    on the lawn dying
cracking up when
you said you would miss
the moon and I
will never forget that
I didn't know what
to say next. You said,
we should never have
gone there, spoils all
the fun in imagining it,
and I thought you meant
to the disco but no
you meant heaven

you never let me be afraid
and so instead I became
a curator. First Mark left
all his records, then you
salvaged Alan's sofa
from his wicked parents.
Arthur asked that you hang on
to his precious baby blue Smith
Corona which you would pass
down to me with your wish:
make something of all this.
I imagined the museum
of all our gone friends
and hated to think
of its stillness: I can't
let you become a statue;
I want them to
remember you
breaking—
at least trying—
into the collection,
dancing away.

the time traveler's waltz [i n t e r l u d e]

the first door I ever fell for was the one Dorothy walked through: you can still see the sepia fading back in the frame as she takes her first steps in technicolor. Kansas behind. A tear in the prairie, and suddenly, you're a little more alive. That's what it feels like— walking through a door. Glass sliders. Brass, Roman bronze. Folding, revolving, rolling back—unhinged— this is what it feels like: a more vivid uncertainty.

Like a Prayer

Every time god closes a door, a gay bar opens.
Last night it was the Stud, dive phoenix rising
from the trash heap, SOMA concrete speckled
with glitter—each piece sure to outlive you or me,
to reflect forever—and drag-teacher Per Sia did
a number where she named all the states
trying to erase us from the records,
(still, the records are ours to spin—)
and they were playing all the hits: *hit me*
baby one more time, bring me a higher love,
and there was a trough of free churros, quesadillas,
because we know how important it is to feed ourselves,
and in the bathroom I noticed the beginnings of
a fresh coat of graffiti, political stickers and wry
one-liners crawling up the black stall walls,
sure to be buried eventually by some future
baby gay's cause, our violence their inheritance,
and next door I heard two queens acting out
a sacred ritual: snort, giggle, kiss, and shit—
the life cycle of nightlife, every dance a sequence
of fabulous repetitions, and if you squint your left eye
just right in San Francisco you'll see our older sisters
moving through the fog, their acts of care echoes

like the chorus on a disco track, and I just read
how Joey Arias climbed into bed with Klaus
Nomi when he was at the end, and blind—
this was 1983, just a short year since the CDC
renamed the so-called *gay plague* the Acquired
Immunodeficiency Syndrome, and nurses in latex left
food for the dying boys at the door—but Joey crept,
under the plastic so he could grab hold the lark,
his friend—and this is what I wish I had told
my student, barely 20 years old, when she gasps,
near tears, that she fears the world is ending
and nobody seems to care, nobody is willing
to face the disaster, every morning it's a shared
consciousness stream litany of man-made atrocity
like sinister petitions, we mumble *hear our prayer*
and feel powerless to gargantuan systems
designed to make us feel powerless,
we weep. The world ends, again, and
we wake up, if we're lucky; I want to
tell her that there's a divine thread that runs
like a velvet rope, keeping all of us in a line
with our ancestors who came before and wept,
and marched against their wars and linked arms
to protect their gay bars and climbed into bed
with their friends, and it's from them that we must
learn how to dance. We are living in a material world,
even if it doesn't feel like it, and touch is the one thing
that cannot be automated. We are living in a material
world and I am a material boy, in that I snort, giggle, kiss,
and shit—in that, I've only got so long to live in this body,
imperfect but enough, and I want to spend my time

on this gorgeous, aching planet singing with my friends.
A voice in the chorus. A fleck of sidewalk glitter, pecked
by a curious pigeon—how they so indiscriminately share
a meal, shared ritual like survival. Two nights ago
Jim drove up the winding hill to Shev's for dinner,
and Shev made custard, Gwyneth Paltrow potatoes,
and a baked chicken recipe from an AIDS cookbook,
called *The Open Hand: Great Chefs Cook for Friends*,
he found in a Palm Springs thrift shop, all the meals
made by sisters, mothers, and, most importantly, friends
when their friends were too frail from wasting to stand
at the kitchen counter, when their friends were too fried
from AZT to make smoothies with various vitamins, roots
and herbs touted as miracle cures—each piece
we eat like a prayer—when their friends were too
tired from dying in the streets, begging polite society
to bear witness to their existence, their friends cooked
this chicken for them, this recipe. This is how we keep
our history; this is how we keep each other alive.
And I've been thinking about how it's going to taste,
heaven, when we get there together—a borderless place
with an eternal banquet table, baked chicken and churros
and a drag queen mouthing along to Klaus Nomi; a gay dive
we've been to a thousand times before to dance, revived.
Our friends, our ancestors, behind us in line—that velvet
rope which keeps us close—we'll laugh about this time
and remember what we made. Remember how we sang.

[/\]

The Palace of Fine Arts Was Built to Look Like a Ruin

and these swans have swum here for a century: two lovebirds,
Blue Boy and Blanche, dubbed by a neighbor who comes daily—
she feeds them dandelion greens. And I keep coming back to you.
At the lagoon, I introduce Blue Boy. Bowing as we go by, me
and you, nameless. We circle. The statues turn their backs
to us, just two more lovers passing through the remains—

and I know I've known you longer than all of this:
1 summer in Damascus, another us eating pomegranate
jewels by the fistful—remember Babylon? We have been
stowaways and sculptors, reluctant soldiers; we have been
here the whole time, men holding one another. Remember
before this was a palace? It was just a bog. It was the fall

of 1990, another you and I came here to say goodbye—
those Levi's once tight and powder blue, now sagging
on your vanishing frame. We gave names to every bird
until finally you were too tired to sit up. It was spring
in 2022: my mother met you, my lover, twice my age,
at the lagoon. She did not know what to call you.

She squeezed my hand and smiled. Blue Boy,
I was the black swan of my family. I flew,

I thought, alone, but we were already here—
as any two lovers passing through a ruin,
at the end of an empire, their embrace
a ripple upon the lake which remains.

The Time Traveler's Bookshelf

is actually a time machine. A ladder
of possibilities. Decades of shelves

and spines, slim poetry slides
next to sculpture, next to geodes;

many parentheses. A wall that is not
a wall, but a door. Always open,

its possibilities always facing you,
begging. An Eden tree in season,

fruit and fruit and fruit, demanding
Bite me. The Time Traveler has to

choose: to ignore a galaxy of futures
and history, or to live with this—

a door that is not a door; it's a painting,
each book a brushstroke. Containing their time.

Suite: A Fraternal Order of Glitter & Ash

The Trojan

A battle is fought, again, in its memory. Its widowed
lovers, and echoes of shells. The songs. Ours was
a war like any other: youthful, private. With time,
I came to remember best that easy summer
just before—he was soft, covered in gold
fuzz, its wiry ends holding each to a drop
of blue as he stepped out from the water—
their recollection, each, a story kept
of their nation, the larger sea;
his calves, the battlefield.
Our age a brutish storm:
courage came to us
piecemeal, and slowly
in its smallest gestures—
dinners after marching,
kissing on the marble steps;
the patchwork spoils of struggle,
our brave and tender intimacy.

The Riot

San Francisco; May 21, 1979

before we drop
our dripping vigil
votives shed hot
white tears
against our knuckles
and his lips
graze my stubble

before the riot
police batons twirl
our temples sideways
he pulls me
close and whispers
let them
call us
anything
but
weak

before he kissed
cement and prayer
wax those lips
gave me language
gave us definition
his love his rage
and reason

before a window
shatters someone

must be left
no choice
my voice
a brick
my name
exploding
your syntax

The Woods

Guerneville; July 4, 1991

Arnold always packed peaches, and Felix booked the room: two queens,
a sleeping roll; you made us laugh the whole way there. At The Woods,
the bunchgrass a pale jade, color of your prized kimono. Arnie palmed
the caps and passed each of us a handful: we'd be floating in no time,

on the floor feeling the Donna Summer and, probably, the mush-
rooms, spinning wildly in the Hexagon to the strings on "Heaven
Knows," pleading for eternity. Far gone. *Believe in us*, you sing, wet
in my ear, and I spin you like a father would his daughter. *We were*

always meant to be, I shout back. That was the night Felix left with
that twink from Sacramento and Arnie threw up in the coffee pot,
so you wiped his collar with club soda and cooed, *sister, just keep*
dancing 'til, in your lap, he fell asleep. The next morning, we died

laughing all the way back to the city, too young for hangovers. When
we did come back without you ten summers later, Donna Summer had
made her big comeback, even if you couldn't. It was feeling like our last

dance, even if we didn't know the next day the entire resort would catch
fire. Redwoods your kimono green, it was the third of July and at least
we finally got rid of Reagan, but none of us felt patriotic, or up for disco

relics, so we sat on the steps of the quiet cabin, us three the old queens
we never wanted to be, eating Arnie's peach galette out of our gooey
palms until we heard the DJ spin Donna's "This Time I Know It's for

Real" for the third time, and by that time Felix felt compelled to get up and move, if only in honor of you, and the night we ate too many 'shrooms and trashed the cabin room. The crowd was thinner,

but we danced, danced, danced until the whole place burned.

The Gay Lunch Table

before PrEP, but just, and after the world
wide web made it easy to catch strange men
in small places, we have so much terrible sex:
my first time; the dog guy; that set designer;

etc.   ASL?   bi   dl   pnp   neg   ddf
we relearn the alphabet. We make up the rules
at our all boys Catholic school lunch table: me,
William, Hunter, Max—our shared language;

lol   omg   *Missouri loves company*
we search in private mode, incognito
window, scrubbing history and the next day
we debrief about what depravity we have seen:

str8 bttm   raw   3some   gay4pay
Will & Grace, Project Runway. We plan our escapes:
Hunter first: to Paris. William, New York. We sneak out
to catch *Brokeback Mountain* on the big screen. We learn

HTML   AIM   mp3   WMV
and how to download illegally. We watch bareback scenes
in a bathroom stall at choir. We march against war but not
for gay marriage; too easy to get caught. We read by flashlight

books on AIDS, ACT UP, DOMA, from the LGBT section
at the library. We hang out there and an all-night diner where
you can still smoke inside. We fill red ash trays, playing grown;
a waiter winks: *a boy like you shouldn't leave his cream behind*;

3:00AM we watch the drag queens come in, cackling. We drive
around all the time: the Jee missing its P; my hail-pitted Mercury;
gold Lady Pilot; we sing sad songs and wish the years to catch
up to us. We drive one another to our internet hookups:

strip mall hotel, suburban house, empty parking lot.
We lie and say we are nineteen because that sounds more
believable. We lie and say we haven't done this before. Lying
back, they say *this was fun*. We turn eighteen. We keep going;

a guy renting someone's damp attic room tells me how
all his friends from high school had died: *the 90s*, he said,
was a different time. I don't know what to do so I hold him
and he sings "I'm On Fire," softly, to me or someone gone,

in the dark. Illegally, I download the song, put it on a CD—
soundtrack to our last summer driving around. Borrowed
memory, how it comes back louder through speakers;
how it changes. By the time we start spreading out

to AUP and NYU and me, to the middle of Missouri,
I start to notice a shift. In the rearview, I still catch it;
how lucky we were to survive all of that. How lucky
we were to survive all of that together.

Rainbow Flag

a love that may endure even past death[1] / / a tenor large and fresh as the creation fills me[2] / / it's true that I've run . . . and run . . . and run . . . [3] / / everyone get out of pulse and keep running[4] / / y'all better quiet down. I've been trying to get up here all day[5] / / y'all come out, come out, my dears[6] / / if you don't flaunt it, who's going to know[7] / / I know the song, I know my opponent, I know the stage, and I know me[8] / / well, at least it's a fruit pie[9] / / I remain who I am, multiple / and one[10] / / we must become muthafuckhas with messages[11] / / just pumping gas and listening to renaissance just having a good time[12] / / that we can still be capable of gestures of loving after lifetimes of all this[13] / / you have to give them hope[14]

1. Justice Anthony Kennedy's majority opinion in the *Obergefell v. Hodges* ruling; 2015.
2. Walt Whitman, *Leaves of Grass*; 1855.
3. Harvey Milk campaign speech on Gay Freedom Day; 1977.
4. Pulse nightclub Facebook post timestamped 2:09am, June 12; 2016.
5. Sylvia Rivera addressing a hostile crowd on Christopher Street Liberation Day; 1973.
6. Patrick Haggerty, *Lavender Country*; 1973.
7. Anita Bryant during a Des Moines television appearance condemning homosexuals; 1977.
8. Sasha Colby performing in a lip sync on *RuPaul's Drag Race*; 2023.
9. Anita Bryant during the same Des Moines television appearance, moments after activist Tom Higgins threw a pie in her face; 1977.
10. Gloria Anzaldúa, *Borderlands/La Frontera: The New Mestiza*; 1987.
11. Assotto Saint, "Why I Write"; 1996.
12. Otis Pena on Facebook Live after witnessing the fatal stabbing of his friend O'Shea Sibley; 2023.
13. David Wojnarowicz, *Close to the Knives: A Memoir of Disintegration*; 1991.
14. Harvey Milk campaign speech on Gay Freedom Day; 1977.

Dancing in the Archives

A proud bronze swirl of asscheeks—
June after June after June, and us
hot pieces of a whole.

Wave to the passing rainbow
parade, princess open-palmed,
from some hungover belvedere

we secured by scrounging
together our meager earnings—
a house on an island named after fire.

Where Frank O'Hara spied his last ever ass.

Banana peels and mango skins
and the sand from that summer or
that next summer stuck, still, in the divots

beneath my combat boots. I am too afraid to go
barefoot at the beach, I do not trust sand,
like how I prefer seeing friends

one-on-one. A piece of the infinity.

Deep in the archive, cruising its dunes
I brush against a stranger's past,
a photograph of a memory of a ghost

dancing, perfectly golden, away from me.

Just then, the parade passes, and I know
someone will have to come after
to sweep up all this glitter,

its little flecks, reflecting back
slices of a perfect sky.
Talking to the sun.

Each piece does not, on its own, flicker.

It's Friday night at the archives and here
I am dancing with my handsome ghosts.
The guy in red shorts from '77,

a couple of blondes rubbing
tanning oil in '81, Mr. Fire
Island of 1990—

each body is not, on its own, a history.

But isn't history made up of records?

And isn't a record also a song?

And when they finally do remember us
they will find us here, dancing
on a beach made of glitter,

a fabulous glitch,
(—weren't we meant to be
erased?—) the memory of a memory,

a disco of echoes. Little mirrors on the ball.

the boys in the angel band [i n t e r l u d e]

Sylvester on vocals
Arthur Russell on the cello
Patrick Cowley mixing
Lance Loud shouting
Klaus Nomi croons
Scott Ross strums harpsichord
Ricky Wilson tuning
Michael Callen a cappella
Assotto Saint commotion
Arnie Zane choreography
Derek Jarman music video
Tseng Kwong Chi photography
David Wojnarowicz theatrics
General Idea sets
Rotimi Fani-Kayode headdress
Keith Haring graffiti
Essex Hemphill recitation
Ray Navarro plays Jesus

A Club Called Heaven

When we finally get to Heaven, the walls shake—heavy bass,
glitter storm. Heaven is a gay bar. Everything is free. Heady pours,

neon beams, the fog. A cloud of synth. Holy Whitney riffs
cascade ever higher, bringing every body upward like hot candy

dripping, there is no roof to hit. Go-go boys in harp-mesh crop tops.
Fistfuls of honey. At the drop, friends crash into friends. Everybody falls

in unison, a fabulous boom. The track starts again. Heaven on repeat,
no curfew. No disease. Everyone has perfect skin. Nobody leaves

the dance floor, a halo of ghosts. Heaven is full of young ghosts.
In line, we press our ears to the wall, listening for a bridge—

Healing the World from Little Island

after Tim Dlugos

Draw a deep breath. Hold it. Let it go.
That's the smell of the Hudson: trash and cargo oil,
another state blinking just across an impossible river. A steel
armature just across the street from the new Whitney
marks the cruising ghosts of Chelsea Street's piers,
my peers in appetite and poor timing, the men
who roamed the run-down docks—leftovers of
an older, less sexy revolution—feeling in the dark
for connection, or coming in masks to photograph
themselves as different men; to mark the breaking walls;
to make something as brief and perfect as an orgasm
last. I breathe the hurried, grateful breaths with these gone
men, artists of necessity. And how much longer will we still
call it the new Whitney? From here, you can spot the green
concrete and lacquered glass towers covering where Sylvia
Rivera lived the last end of her historic life in a tent. I split my time
unevenly between two centuries, straddling crises like Manhattan—
on a day as blue as this, who could forget the suited men sailing
through the sky, the paper flying, coughing up smoke—yes, but
let's not forget, too, the flyers and the food banks and the Union
Square vigil. Where is the memorial to the people who helped
each other down the stairs? May the breath I draw become
a spotlight to beckon back all the displaced souls

from all the disaster zones: the evicted, the convicted,
the pockmarked and the bullet wounded, the native and
the immigrant; all my friends. Anyone who dances along
the tulip edges of a man-made island. I split my time
between what I can see in front of me and the screen, a piece
of glass obstructing my view so that my heart breaks twice
with each injustice: once for feeling, once for feeling powerless.
In the Just-Before Times I marched right up that avenue,
in the opposite direction of Pride, with thousands of angry
strangers holding signs calling for resistance. I came alone,
but I made friends and by the end of the night I was dancing
with the Sisters of Perpetual Indulgence to "Heart of Glass"
in a rent-controlled rat's nest above Christopher Street
where the parade just kept passing by and I split my time
in pieces like a busted tiara for every queen who gave me strength
to keep moving. This breath is for all the dashed dreams of that before
and for how many have had to sit through this plague in one room,
how many have had to work through this plague in emergency rooms,
in supermarkets, on mass transit—glasses fogging up on masked buses,
balancing baskets of someone else's dinner on a bicycle—and for those
moments, too, of true connection: playing "I Will Survive" for passersby
on our roof, scooping out bowls of perpetual stew. I split my time
between emergencies and the spaces of peace which live inside
each of them. Hurricane eyes of community, random acts of beauty
that go unreported, but are as real as the damage. I breathe in
the powerless, the priced-out, the tent cities and the artists;
the disparate young desperate for a real experience. And each
grain of sand on the beach spills out from a busted hourglass;
we feel it all. But we do not yet know its name. Like Quakers,
we wait silently for the words to reveal themselves—
but what if there are no words? What if there is only light?

I breathe in, and release a beam bright enough to reveal
the ghosts sucking each other off in the empty monument,
illuminate their fleeting love, shine on the loudmouth activists
and outspoken poets buried under the rubble of the greater West
Village, a light so bright it breaks time, splits the day like an egg,
freeing those who've gone and those to come from the emerald
glass-and-steel skyline as it dissolves into sand. Little bits of past
and future love slipping together in a glow. This is a moment
of lightness you can hold in the palm of your hand—
its essence catches in your life line; feel it writhe.
Hold on to this as long as you can.

[\]

The Time Traveler Finally Falls in Love

and it ends, of course, in fabulous heartbreak, like anything—
it's not an if, but when—so the trick is learning how to bend
the days you get: nailing our flowers to the wall, reading
side by side; memorize his body curving like a question
mark, asking, can we stay like this forever? We can.
We travel to his boyhood home; to ancient Rome; to
my twenties where we laugh at what I thought was real
love; we see art in every century. We grow old together
at different times. We rebuild our ship from scraps
of former relationships—debris of who we have
been or seen, blueprints for our future past. We host
our friends for cocktail hours. We sign a lease on a house.
I meet his friends, and through them, I love him more. I take
him to his first drag show. He talks us through our first fight;
we have the same fight again. We kiss on corners just because
we have fought hard for it. We make up words for this. I say,
I have never been in love. I ask, how will I know what's next?
He takes my hand. He takes me home. We meet, as strangers,
on a blank morning, and he says he doesn't have much time.
Instantly, I recognize this man. I've been waiting here for him.

Heirloom

We won't have any children,
we'll have dinner
reservations with friends.

We will leave
behind only bodies
of art, letters—

not even letters—
text exchanges. Heirloom
tomato vines, hydrangeas

and coyote mint.
We will arrange
friends to water

our beds, our oleanders
when we travel, trading
favors. We will stay

home and go
days without calls, then
suddenly everyone wants

to get together—
we'll always say yes.
We will have built

this brood—our own—
from the ground
up: old friends,

their lovers, us
and the tomatoes.
We will continue

tending new fruits
every summer: moonwashed
suppers, light entertainment,

a place to stay. We will change
together and alone, plump
tomatoes sharing a vine.

We will grow
a history of exchanges
made with friends:

lemons for sculptures
or books, our pieces
they will have to keep.

A Little Door

Nothing stays dead long. Sonoma
yellow pine, the memory of a Saturday
hardware store aroma. Sawdust and dads.
Quiet up north. Only sound is the thumping
bass from bears in rainbow inner tubes, lazing
down the Russian River. The power blows
but the music doesn't stop. They must have
a generator. Low-battery mode, we check
our phones to make sure there is not a fire.
You have a lantern. You make a promise
you will keep me safe tonight. It turns
out that—this—is what I needed.
We needed to cover up
our medicine chest,
so you made a little door.
It's out there, drying. I make a plan
to grab it if we have to run. A door you
built with your own two hands—we will
find or make a hole that needs it.

clock.wrk// (the time traveler's loop) [i n t e r l u d e]

[| / /]
with what we have
lost we dance

[| /]
toward a fabulous either
one man is now another

[/]
the only way we know
to move is on

[|]
with each loss I am learning
how to dance

[/ /]
toward both
a fabulous either

[/ |]
another tired binary
forward and backward

[/ / /]
forward and backward
another tired binary

[\ / / /]
one man's now is another man's
past or future

[/ \ ]
to move on is
the only way we know

[\ / /]
we mourn what we have
come to know as now

[\ ]
with each step I am learning
how to mourn

[\ /]
lost we dance
with what we have

Starman

The night that David Bowie died I went out dancing
in some downtown gay bar, crying, *Is there life on*
Mars? Another question I had once asked Dad
in the car: do you remember this one? Naturally,

when someone famous dies, they leave so many images
behind: young David, reclined, on the *Hunky Dory* cover;
Ziggy Stardust; the Thin White Duke. As for my father,
I only have a few: polaroid of a black-and-white cowboy,

beaming before a silver tree; a student ID, scholarship kid
studying English in Ottawa, Kansas—his hair 1970s long
and golden, big yellow smile; Dad in plaid bell bottoms
with his niece Denise, their open hands outstretched,

and singing; Dad in costume: the Jester, in King Henry's
Feast—his leap from waiter to actor in a dinner theater;
Dad with the big Martin on his lap, playing me a song.
Tuesday drives to guitar lessons we used to only listen

to old albums. I would quiz him on the past: what song
was at number one on the day of the moon landing?
Where were you? Did you watch? How did it feel?
"Changes," one time, blasting, I wanted to know—

Bowie's gay, right? Dad answered, plainly, *well, no.*
But what about his makeup? I pressed. His clothes,
how he moves. *Oh, that's just Bowie*, Dad smiled.
He's just how he is. That's it. No joke, no warning

against my wondering. I don't know if he knew
how much it meant to me that he didn't laugh.
We drove, like every Tuesday, the long way
home, listening together, singing along.

Saturn Street Steps

The spot where we sit/sat and you hold
/held me /let me go
looks out all across [what used to be]
Eureka Valley: little diamond tips,
the pastel Victorians /sand dunes /glass
skyscrapers. We must [have]
look [ed] so tiny when
you take/took
my hand in your fist
and tell/told
me how long it would last—
the memory of the feeling of being
so briefly, perfectly alive: for all time.
and I laugh [ed], nervously or
because I know/knew even now/then
how right you are/were. We kiss
[ed] /release
and under us the city
comes/came back
to life. For a moment, it is/was called
San Francisco
but this hill was here before us
and it is/will be here [still] long after
we leave. /we are gone.
/we return.

The Time Traveler Meets Themselves

When I first see myself, we recall skipping
US history—god, we were so high then
on freedom; I lived to regret it. Rebel me,
braver than I knew. On a bright glacier, we
embrace. Under us, just ice. We form ourselves

into a circle, teeth chattering. Baby me, now
me, the me I have yet to formally meet—an us
convention on a blank icecap. We chit-chat.
The smallest one asks the right questions:
How does it feel to dance backward?

Which one of us will remember all of this?
My twenties, they are proud, talking nonstop
with my old man, who looks equally unafraid.
A kaleidoscope of monarchs flies overhead
and in this moment, we all turn to wave:

their wings, an orange flicker like film
reel, pushing away the white sky. See,
we each get such a small lifetime
to know exactly what we are—
and then we change again.

I glance back, and my rebel drifts
off into the frozen past, laughing,
having learned nothing, doomed
to make the same fabulous mistakes,
and I guess I will have to do the same.

[ ]

Anderson Cooper Interviews the Time Traveler

This interview was conducted in Aug. 2019 for the American television program 60 Minutes. *It has been transcribed and condensed for clarity here.*

Anderson Cooper: Welcome, welcome . . . back? I guess I should say.

Time Traveler: Thank you, it's a long trip. Makes the flight to Sydney feel like a spa day. But I'm very happy to be here.

AC: Now, you've been both celebrated and criticized for your long careers in every arena from pop music to prospecting to war. For those who are unfamiliar with your broad resume, how would you describe what it is you do?

TT: Like everyone, I am a doorway. I just don't have a door.

AC: You've resisted being referred to as a *queer* Time Traveler, telling the Times, and I'm quoting you, "I am older than labels and too young to pin down."

TT: That's actually mischaracterized, it's the *time traveler* label I'm resisting. Nobody should be so defined by their work. Please, let the record show I am proudly, historically queer.

AC: Does it feel important for you to say that?

TT: Right now? In this century? In this dire, fabulous moment? Yes. Very.

AC: You had a hit in 1977 with the song "Take Me Back (In Time)" you produced with Patrick Cowley, and I just want to read some of the lyrics here . . .

TT: Oh boy.

AC: "Baby, let's just let this end, so we can go back to the start... Take me back, take me back in time, let's finish at the start . . . " and I don't think I can read the next double entendre on CBS.

TT: It was the seventies.

AC: Do you find it difficult to find love when you . . .

TT: I've found the hardest thing about love, in my experience, is being open to the joy inside of a moment you know is just an interlude between disasters.

AC: You feel stuck between joy and disaster?

TT: [*Laughs*] Don't you? Don't we all? That's what makes the best stuff good—that it ends— You can look forward to it and you can look back on it but you can't get your hands around love. It comes on like weather.

AC: Have you found that your queerness has made that more difficult?

TT: It's funny, I was at dinner the other night with John [Chaffee] and Jason [Chamberlain], they came out to California in [18] '49—looking for gold; and they found it—and they've lived out toward Yosemite, together, for nearly half a century. Lovely couple. There's a real tenderness there, in this little world they made for themselves.

You know, in our century we like to think we were the ones that figured everything out. But we've still got plenty to learn. And we've got models both directions who have been loving and fighting and dreaming up and surviving for lifetimes.

AC: I read somewhere you had been considering retiring. What does that look like for you?

TT: Staying in one place, I guess. I mean, one timeline.

AC: Where—or, when—would that be?

TT: Oh, I've thought about the Renaissance, the Hot Romantic—we're getting there—you know, Athens. But honestly, I know this is so boring, but I think I'd stay here.

AC: Is this the best time to be alive?

TT: The best? [*Laughs*] No, no time is better or worse than any other. This idea, that everything moves forward . . . We want progress to be linear, but it's more like a wheel. Hope is seasonal. So no matter what era you're in, there's dancing and there's disease.

AC: I'm sure some viewers would argue that that's not so simple if you're Black in the nineteenth century, or if you're a Japanese American in the 1940s, or—

TT: Exactly! No, I mean, here we are in the accumulation of so much more perspective, and it's wonderful and it feels like it's the end of the world. But of course it's not. There's no endings! Only change. Only a gorgeous, awful change.

AC: So you were recently visiting the 22nd century, can you share with us—are you even allowed to?—share anything we should be looking out for?

TT: There's nothing that we do not already have, or know. There is nothing coming that cannot already be imagined.

AC: Sounds ominous.

TT: No, it's a powerful thing. Whatever's next, we're dreaming up right now. I could tell you all the bad stuff, but you already know—yes, there's plague and fire and frogs and darkness. Of course. But close your eyes and think of what else—what are the beautiful parts, the new freedoms and songs you haven't heard and better ways to love? See it? There's all that, too.

The Time Traveler Moves On

and on the next track I want to
unlearn everything and begin
this time a fabulous dancer
I want to trip light with my sister
pass down history by fluttering hips
flux my calves to cause a melody
start and finish a revolution
to be played in song is to be made
a future ancestor means to be made to last louder
I want to throw my body like a party
into the hard earth one more worm
dancing under a grave once more
time wiggle and endure
I want to come back shorter
just a beat between beats
or a bolt as it slides electric
from the silver prick of a needle
across the record's deep grooves
I want to stretch our record longer
so I can learn from my sister the moves
each step a loss to mourn
each step a future too

Acknowledgments

Nobody really dances alone. I am grateful for the sharp eyes and warm hearts of my brilliant friends, whose support has been essential in bringing me to this moment: Chip Miller & Hunter Capps & Max Pluenneke, my history, my fates; Patrick Haggerty (who we all miss) & JB, who taught us how to love; Kyle Grelle & Nacho de la Higuera; Nora Salle, for giving me L-I-F-E after all these years; Michael Shymanski, who makes my DIY publishing dreams come true, & Jim McGowan, who gave me *Cruising Utopia*; Anna Boisseau, who had the brilliant idea that I go back to school, & Iavora Vlaytcheva, who helped get me there; Darrian O'Reilly who taught me to dance; Moll Caffey, for the links and webs, & Benny Johnson, for their vision; Fritz Hutchison & Al Hawkins for making "Love Song" sing; Dillon McRoberts & Mary Fama, & Brooklyn; Zac Jurden; Moss Bellm; Anne Danielski; Sav Stephenson, & our gay schemes; Rita Burke; Genevieve Brummel; Paige Pritchard; Evan Wood; Katherine Morgan, how we'd dream up our future books; Jon Taylor, for his books, & Tom Heidel; Marissa Wolf, Charles Grant, Tom Toro, for throwing our dreams into the fire; Kevin Bentley, the wild animal; Vitaly Chernetsky, for your translations; Wayne Bund, for capturing movement, color, and light; James Spindler & John Vitale, for your words and music; Tina V. Aguirre & Bill Jennings; Carol Vena-Mondt, for endless insight; Adam Possehl & Marcus Ewert & Kar Johnson & all the other booksellers; Julian Morris & Michael-Vincent D'Anella-Mercanti; Brendan McHugh, my sister-writer, & Thomas Kurtz, my sister-teacher; David Gilbert, John Burtle, Daniel Arthur Mendoza who make worlds in their work; Kevin Bertolero, William Ward Butler, London Pinkney, Chad Koch & Miah Jeffra, Ben Townley-Canning who give poetry a place; & Thea Frost, my daring partner in art.

The poems in this collection were distinctly shaped by my fellow poets in the University of San Francisco MFA program: Cal Calamia & Samantha Stevens & KC Crawford & Katie Tomzynski & Alison Zheng & Neda Sarrami & Alex Hutton; Sarah E. Kruse & Leonel Sánchez Lopez & Sydney Vogl, thank you for crying with me; Saranya Subramanian, Neal Tayco, Calaghan Rowley, Bobbie Quinn & Tanya Žilinskas, I'm so grateful we got the chance to sing together. My immense gratitude to the generosity and generative guidance extended by my teachers: Maw Shein Win, Alan Chazaro, K.M. Soehnlein, MK Chavez, & Susan Steinberg. To the poets, too, who I met along the way: Aaron Shurin, David Trinidad, Laura Weatherington, Maggie Queeney, Randall Mann, Amanda Moore, Mukethe Kawinzi; Hieu Minh Nguyen, & sam sax. Special thanks to Preeti Vangani, whose care with the first pass at this project helped it find its voice—and its title!—and to D.A. Powell, whose disco wisdom was instrumental in shaping this work.

Another Anthem of Fabulous Survival is dedicated my father, Michael, who never got the chance to finish his book. Without his model of compassion and curiosity, I may never have attempted to write my own. My cousins, aunts, uncles never turned me away: a too-rare gift. My mother, Mary, and my sister, Emily, especially, have offered boundless encouragement as I pursue my most unlikely dreams. I know how lucky I am to learn from their love.

Finally, for Jim Isermann—my first reader and my last kiss—I wouldn't have known the ending if I hadn't known your love. Turns out, there is no end. Only more to make.

My deepest gratitude to the editors of the following publications in which these poems or earlier versions first appeared:

& Change: "Love Song"

Bridge: "Healing the World from Little Island"; "clock.wrk//"

Door is a Jar: "The Time Traveler Meets Themselves"

Foglifter: "'Halo'"

Fourteen Poems: "A National Anthem"

Frontera: "*[. . . and coming upon the cave . . .]*"

Frozen Sea: "Starman"

Miracle Monocle: "The Gay Lunch Table"

Poetry: "Instructions for Building Your First Time Machine"; "The Time Traveler Finally Falls in Love"

Post Road: "Saturn Street Steps"

The Racket: "Earth, Wind, and Mostly Fire"; "Fairyland"

The San Franciscan: "A Little Door"

The Seaford Review: "The Trojan"

Thanks to Meg Day, a beacon, for seeing in this work something worth celebrating. Their poetic brilliance and literary citizenship have long been a model, and I'm so proud to dance along their line.

Thanks to the fabulous Elisabeth Frost for her stewardship of the Poetic Justice Institute. Her tender attention has been crucial in making this dream a reality. Thanks to Tim Roberts for his careful reading. Thanks to everyone at Fordham University Press, especially Richard Morrison and Kate O'Brien-Nicholson, for shepherding this book into the world. I crashed into the right place.

The edited text in "Operating Manual for the Time Traveler" comes from the LM/AGS Operating Manual, Flight Program 6, July 1969—it is sourced from NASA's Apollo Lunar Surface Journal.

The images in "Anderson Cooper Interviews the Time Traveler" include an empty Columbia Records 12" disco single sleeve, sourced from *The Art of Cover Art*, as well as a photograph of John Chaffee and Jason Chamberlain sourced from the *Online Archive of California*.

This book's epigraph comes from the CAConrad poem "If No One Comes to Save You It's Because of Television," found in their collection *Ecodeviance: (soma)tics for the Future Wilderness* (Wave Books, 2014).

The cover image is a 1984 photograph by Jean-Baptiste Carhaix of Sister Dominique Nique-Nique at the Marin Headlands. Carhaix was a French photographer who, during summers in San Francisco, became first fascinated by, then devoted to, the Sisters of Perpetual Indulgence, recognizing in these alternative nuns a brave ministry that they performed for those suffering in the early ravages of the HIV/AIDS epidemic. He took a series of posed portraits with the Sisters as models at the Headlands, the spires of San Francisco glimpsed, barely, in the fogged background.

Thank you to Angela Moody for so beautifully bringing the cover design to life.

Thanks to Devin McGeehan Muchmore, the Managing Reference Archivist at the GLBT Historical Society—where Carhaix's work is collected—for facilitating its use, and to all the other archivists, staff, and volunteers at the Historical Society.

None of this work would exist without our lovingly tended LGBTQ+ archives. For these poems I found material and inspiration in the collections of the GLBT Historical Society, the ONE Archives at the USC Libraries, the LGBT Community Center National History Archive, the Daniel E. Koshland San Francisco History Center at San Francisco Public Library, the New York Public Library's LGBTQ+ Collection, and the Gay and Lesbian Archive of Mid-America. Along a lineage of poetry and music, archives and ephemera, there is a simultaneous, joyous index of us. It is a history of celebration and struggle, of revelatory movement; it is also a future.

We have always been [t]here.

We are not [ever] going anywhere.

We are/were everywhere and we are/were not afraid.

Keep singing, loud enough so they can hear us all the way to tomorrow.

T.S. Leonard is a poet, performer, and educator whose work has been featured in *Poetry*, *Foglifter*, *Fourteen Poems*, and in collaborative projects at the Portland Art Museum and Pacific Design Center. Originally from Kansas City, Missouri, he lives and teaches in San Francisco.

POETIC JUSTICE INSTITUTE

Diana Keren Lee

How to Cast a Beautiful Animal

T.S. Leonard

Another Anthem of Fabulous Survival

foreword by Meg Day

Adedayo Agarau

The Years of Blood

Marcella Durand

A Winter Triangle

foreword by Srikanth Reddy

POETS OUT LOUD

Prize Winners

Jennifer Atkinson, *A Gray Realm the Ocean*

Alison Powell, *Boats in the Attic*

Stephanie Ellis Schlaifer, *Well Waiting Room*

Sarah Mangold, *Her Wilderness Will Be Her Manners*

José Felipe Alvergue, *scenery: a lyric*

S. Brook Corfman, *My Daily Actions, or The Meteorites*

Henk Rossouw, *Xamissa*

Julia Bouwsma, *Midden*

Gary Keenan, *Rotary Devotion*

Michael D. Snediker, *The New York Editions*

Gregory Mahrer, *A Provisional Map of the Lost Continent*

Nancy K. Pearson, *The Whole by Contemplation of a Single Bone*

Daneen Wardrop, *Cyclorama*

Terrence Chiusano, *On Generation & Corruption*

Sara Michas-Martin, *Gray Matter*

Peter Streckfus, *Errings*

Amy Sara Carroll, *Fannie + Freddie: The Sentimentality of Post–9/11 Pornography*

Nicolas Hundley, *The Revolver in the Hive*

Julie Choffel, *The Hello Delay*

Michelle Naka Pierce, *Continuous Frieze Bordering Red*

Leslie C. Chang, *Things That No Longer Delight Me*

Amy Catanzano, *Multiversal*

Darcie Dennigan, *Corinna A-Maying the Apocalypse*

Karin Gottshall, *Crocus*

Jean Gallagher, *This Minute*

Lee Robinson, *Hearsay*

Janet Kaplan, *The Glazier's Country*

Robert Thomas, *Door to Door*

Julie Sheehan, *Thaw*

Jennifer Clarvoe, *Invisible Tender*

www.ingramcontent.com/pod-product-compliance
Lightning Source LLC
LaVergne TN
LVHW101925280826
846781LV00021B/189